Umbra

ALSO BY
ERIC BASSO
FROM
ASYLUM ARTS PRESS

FICTION
The Beak Doctor
Bartholomew Fair

POETRY
Accidental Monsters
The Catwalk Watch
The Smoking Mirror
Catafalques
Ghost Light

DRAMA
Enigmas
The Golem Triptych
The Sabattier Effect

ESSAYS
Decompositions

BOOK OF DREAMS
Revagations

FROM
SIX GALLERY PRESS

POETRY
Earthworks

ERIC BASSO

Umbra

Poems
1976-1977

ASYLUM ARTS PRESS RALEIGH ⊕ 2010

Copyright © 1977, 2010 by Eric Basso

All rights reserved. No part of this publication may be reproduced or transmitted in any form or by any means, electronic or mechanical, including photocopy, recording, or any information storage and retrieval system, without permission in writing from the publisher, except for brief quotes in reviews.

Some of these poems first appeared in *Blackbird* and *Juxta*, to whose editors grateful acknowledgement is made.

ISBN-13:   978-1-878580-72-6
Library of Congress Control Number: 2009939002

Basso, Eric, 1947–
Umbra

1. Basso, Eric — Poetry.
2. Authors, American — 20th Century — Poetry.

Printed in The United States of America.

Cover illustration by the author (1977).

FIRST EDITION

Asylum Arts Press
An imprint of LDP Media, LLC
PO Box 90473
Raleigh, NC 27675-0473
www.leapingdogpress.com

for
DAVID STONE

Celui qui voit l'absurde
souffre ce supplice: avoir
le Mot-de-la-fin-de-tout
sur le bout de la langue,
mais imprononçable.

≽ René Daumal

Contents

Limbus

Match Key	5
Eugavague	6
Somnvs	7
Interface	8
Lost Methodology	9
Devil Dream	10
Melodisdream	11
Moths	12
Darkroom	13
Bluebeard's Dream	14
Habitude	15
Capharnaüm	16
Homecoming	17
Bottled Depths	18
Promenade	19
The Course	20
Cuttering	21
The Prey	22
Anti-Static Laws	23
Catechlysm	24
At the Office	25
Descent	26
Disturbance	27
Photographs	28
Tar	29

Little Theatre	30
Permeation	31
Raccrocs	32
Elephant Circus	33
Longdistance	34
Memento	35
Harbor Lights	36
White Night	37
White Deserts	38
Sleep	39
Claque	40
Galleries	41
Orient	43
At Twilight	44
Celles	45
The Exhibit	46
Chamber Music	47
Natural Gas	48
Neglect	49
Traveler	50
Portraits	51
Pelican Test	52
Kestrels	53
Bureauc Rat	54
Book Worm	55
Container	56
The Other Frankenstein	57
Batik	58
Collector	59
Nostalgia	60
Scene of the Crime	61
Omicron	62

Recluse	63
The Webs	64
Of Mutes	65
Idiotics	66
The Search for Napoleon	67
Renard	68
Ennui	69
Mnemes	71
Plankton	72
O	73
The Benediction	74
Last Kinetoscope	75
Drunk	76
Impression	77
Nightschool	79
Vigil	80
Legend	81
Orb	82
Properties	83
Blue Heron Inn	85
Toe to Toe	86
Romantic Opium	88
Cinema	90
Hypnotics	92
Germination	93
Man in a Pond	94
Osteology	96
Unfinished Diesel	97
Worm Wood	98
Nautilus	99

Histories

Rumor	103
To Conjure	104
The Seven Shades	105
Monody	106
Piscivm	107
Covered Bridge	108
Luna	109
Hincha	110
The Silents	111
Soma	112
Kells	114
La Complainte Ylvain	115
Hog Tender	116
Artisan	117
Dante to Enamel	118
The Plague	119
The Conqueror's Horse	120
Chivalric Legend	121
Merlin	122
Guelphs	123
The Recompense	124
Astrolabe	125
Watchman	126
The Moorish Horse	127
The Assassins	129
Peregrination	130
Carnaval Ending	131
Winter	132
Obeah	133

Amnesia	134
Bivouac	135
Crawl Space	136
Quadrant	137
The Captive	138
Herbal	139

Occasions

Arcology	143
Phantom	144
October Nights	145
Elevations	146
The Shore	147
Expectation	148
Apparatus	149
Lent	150
A Rheum for the Night	151
The Dead Fish	152

Memoirs

Protozoa	157
Red Weather	158
My Room at 8 O'Clock	160
Cricketing	161
Cuckold	162
Jorgue	163
Pairs	165
Clockwork	166

Outside a Library	167
In the Hôtel Orfila	168
Polydor in Bed	169
Dead Letter	170
Rorschach	171
Eclipse	172
Aftermath	173
Sideshow	174
Sadness	175
Tango Mask	176
Water Mark	177
Modifications	178
Feeding	179
Reliquary	180
Album	181
Exergue	182
Apprentice	183
The Ending	184
Crevass	185
Bal	186
Repository	187
Eaters	188
Arrival	189
Women	190
Haunted	191
Trist	192
Possessions	193
Erasure	194
Decor	195
The Thing	197
Pluvians	198
Aphid	199

After the Journey	200
Orcq	201
Isle	202
Gothick Recess	203
A General's House	204
The Night Before	205
Specimen Teeth	206
The Other Voice	207
Portmanteau	208
Sync Dying	209
The Toll	210
Numbers	211
Sundering	213
Palace of Hong Kong	214
Cyclostome	215
Memoirs	216

This Side of the Silence

The Bottom Page	219
An Imitation Light	221
The Synthesis	222
The March	223
Settings	224
Blem	225
Balloon Gondola	226
Feline	227
Orpheus Rocker	228
Recall	229
Before the Switch	230

Cartograph	231
Rites	232
Moon-Blind	233
Moments	234
Exhaustion	235
Fireside Audience	236
Fzzz	237
The Box	238
Gemian	239
Parallels	240
Etiquette	241
Nemesis	242
Echo	243
The Medium	244
Inside	245
An Anecdote	246
Doubling	247
Excavation	248
Someone	249
Limn	250
Towards Midnight	252
Haze Elegy	253
Witness	254
Eviction	256
The Baths	258
Cow Catchers	260
The Diva	261
To The Ruin	262
Interregnum	263
Locusts	264
The Zone	266
Fading Algebra	267

The Recognition	268
Topology	269
Vox Umbra	270

Umbra

Limbus

Match Key

the pattern
flare-light

curvilinear
distortions

a
broken lens
these
dimming lan
tern-slides
unyolk with
in a glassy
orbit

the rain is
falling

December 7, 1976

Eugavague

rats on a
small is-
land into
the smoke

it passes

turns fog
to clink-
ering fog

this crew
of ghosts
in shapes
that come
and go in
the night

November 18, 1976

Somnvs

all things come at
night you have on-
ly to lid your eye
interior paradoxes
lashes a blur that
focuses all middle
distant objects in
a room just before
you drift off into
images phosphenes-
cing tumors in the
shadows hollow out
tunnels into dream

August 17, 1976

Interface

with the last

places a spi-
der would not
want to touch
with its webs

once you have
begun to fall
through a few
black mirages
you let go of
everything in
the room that
might suggest
you are awake

December 18, 1976

Lost Methodology

    each saw a huge eye
    from the other side
     of the judas-hole
    a beat then a move-
    ment of dead leaves
    that might be wings

    to re-create an owl
    they took the night
    in little doses one
    glance at a time on
    longforgotten trees

    but through a cabi-
    net of dark mirrors

July 26, 1976

Devil Dream

you can see
them if you
strain your
eyes in the
wormy dark-
ness of the
kitchen

the hound's
teeth

you go down
without the
light

crawling to
escape from
the sleeper

November 21, 1976

Melodisdream

the pose is familiar

mousered hair frizzening
a small halo against the
light around her shrunk-
en scalplock *pas de deux*

crossed ankles above the
mercury-vapor bath where
the dead are silvering

I come into the twilight
vomitorium on tip-toe to
draw the blind

August 24, 1976

Moths

her face is there among oth
ers we have tried to forget

from a dark fleck spreading
its wings across the sherry
amber to the lampshade-flut
ter traps laid for these dy
ing insects clutter the rug

we pick them up at night un
der the monastery ruins old
cobwebbed cocoons lodged in
a wall of desiccating heads

August 23, 1976

Darkroom

once she
had lips

and fin-
gernails
she took
hours to
 polish

kissed
them all
good bye

for this
bloodred
darkness
of the
lamp

February 6, 1977

Bluebeard's Dream

a quarter to midnight cake and
ale rolling in barrels beneath
the hull of this deserted ship

Bluebeard before the last door
where they kept the hardboiled
eggs

a passage home behind the gas-
flames in an iron grille as if
he had begun the journey under
a delusion

September 5, 1976

Habitude

    to read
    these words
        unlock

    through
    the pages of
      a diary

  the dust
  with your finger
       tips

  find a key
  to shut up the
     library

January 31, 1977

Capharnaüm

stay just long enough to
feel the tiles drop away
beneath your unshod feet

woman who wraps her hair
in a towel will come out
of your room at midnight
and lead you down by the
hand through the dark at
the top of the staircase

and I will wait here for
you to find the way back

October 6, 1976

Homecoming

she takes her positiom
behind the tassels you
catch a whiff of lutes

a head lowered between
the bedposts listening
for a small squeak in-
 side the wallpaper

tracks
smudges of silk remain
of an intimate
friend

one last
lost caterpillar

November 10, 1976

Bottled Depths

he followed always

the few paces more
behind her nothing
would diminish the
distance of carpet
grass thinning out
into dunes and the
dunes into clouded
watery catacombs

a city within this
hall of blue doors

somewhere he would
find his abandoned
hovel only to lose
all trace of her
footprints

April 21, 1977

Promenade

here
where the hand is
nothing but a tis
sue of unraveling
             lines
in search of
the way back down
through the masks
      of sand
and wormeaten
timberboards into
an unending sleep
he liked
to go poking with
the rubber tip of
        his cane
pushing it
in up to the root
of its wickerwork
        handle

September 15, 1976

The Course

two ladies tugged down
their hatbrims on what
passed for the fall of
night for in that time
and place such a thing
as dusk was an unknown
passing of the seasons
by word and gesture so
obscure that no one in
his right mind stopped
to lend interpretation
and the sun long years
was lost to memory

March 30, 1977

Cuttering

old woodcut fly
a ghost with the neck
    of dying swans

Lohengrin pedals
his ferry across this
  sinking everglade
  to where the moss
   is like a new
    mown carpet

gazing
with an eye closed on
the image of his iris
  pupil and lashes
   three sheets to
      the wind
in his monocle

February 17, 1977

The Prey

    this place of repose
more than just another
cellar room
        underneath
   the grid is part
of a ghost town in the
grass
      we forage for
the mammoth cranes
buried here before the
flood

   some are still alive
and call us to the dig
ging with their
      half-smothered
      beaks

April 15, 1977

Anti-Static Laws

a doze or
was it *Oh my god
there is a mastodon
         in the cellar!*

what then?
I don't feel
much like sleeping
                now

at least the bones
a small bag of bones
     by the wine cask
*the two of us
are never far from
                it*

what was it
you said last night?
         something
         about a search
         for missing
         webs?

zzzzzzzzzzzzzz etc.

March 3, 1977

Catechlysm

what makes the mummy laugh?
green ramparts gone to seed
behind the garbage cans

    and his mother?
    nothing anymore
    she crapped out
    before we could
    get her answer

    the family ibis?
    without form and
    void an unsolved
    moon at the edge
    of the ecliptic

        who waits?
        an unknown

July 20, 1976

At the Office

the aged fœtus
curled up under
a roll-top desk

of doubtful sex
his souvenir of
time long pick-
led in a filthy
jar

frog face to an
obtuse formalin
cloud

March 14, 1977

Descent

the green be-
hind her eyes
and images of
plaster walls
about to drop
away into no-
thing where a
bark waits to
take her down
the canal

waterworks of
all the murky
reflections a
shade lighter
than aquablue

to the bottom
of the cave

December 2, 1976

Disturbance

soft the din of
a dragging heel

no rest for the
insomniacs with
plaster falling
in a cloud over
their mummified
faces

we hear the old
men are walking
up in the attic

March 10, 1977

Photographs

what the emulsion
keeps of its fine
silver dust

the rest may come
up in the bromide

is just enough to
turn this ceiling
black

up to weak lights
the image hangs

the fuse sets off
white oxide fila-
ments burned into
rungs of a jacobs
ladder in mid-air

the last to die

November 14, 1976

Tar

and the crows
made it dance
like a puppet
on the wind

stakes shaggy
bundles above
pitchblende

a dead weight
pulls it into
the horizon

March 11, 1977

Little Theatre

upside down in
the foyer what
neither breath
nor a wind can
move above the
old chandelier
calmly spreads
its wings like
nameless shad-
ows across the
puppet faces a
last whimsical
smile brings
down the Man
in the
Moon

December 6, 1976

Permeation

separation
  from the light hiss
  invisible membranes
and in the ripples a
crackle of electrons
line by line across
the screen
                thin
  splinters of glass
  caught between the
  lampposts glitter-
  ing static unmakes
      the shadowed
           face
within
the photographs

April 29, 1977

Raccrocs

meadows roll off
broad clusters
toward a cloud
of minuscule
dots

from the first
to the last pedaller
a tandem equilibrium
of flags at halfmast
in the afternoon
by $crooge's
moneybin

March 25, 1977

Elephant Circus

    these footprints
    not an idea left in the mud
      to fill them up again with
                  rainwater

    our resistance
    so slow by night
    that through a tear
    in this canvas pyramid dark
     shapes other than our own
       might lie in the sawdust
        ready to close the eyes
         of mammoth sleepers
    with a handful of sand
    or with what the footprints
            have left behind

April 5, 1977

Longdistance

for David Ziskin

an upstairs corridor
crossing the mirrors

sail-pitched glances
in this bedroom lake

a pelican goes sound
lessly under the rug

glances on the grill
in bluetipped flames

a telephone was ring
ing calling her away

September 3, 1976

Memento

for Ron Dolezal

the grove rusts a
gainst its embers
on the windowpane
remember the dead

the spinningwheel
behind them in an
alcove lit by the
pines

three men in wigs
by an open window
gazing out of the
firescreen at the
plummeting leaves

September 1, 1976

Harbor Lights

for Neil Bobrick

feverdreams in fog a claustrophobic
music draws its wooden zombies from
the night with a mellow tenor voice

faceless under the Chinese lanterns
waters where the moon sinks down in
slivers of liquid metal the puppets
are waltzing after a lost nostalgia
of pomaded hair and satin crinoline
in eyeless couples two by two alone
on a terrace through the dull mists
turning round in one another's arms
to the tune of longforgotten lights

September 13, 1976

White Night

    push the bramble
aside nettle-thorns
under the blizzard-
window skylights in
the underbrush

    the maze of streets
my caravan retraces

    the wooden bulkhead
you can almost hear

    staggered lampposts
on the median open-
light
    on a tumbledown
café half-buried in
the snow

April 26, 1977

White Deserts

      they take you
      down
           one eye
      to the screen
      of ice
      in a darkened
           elevator
      relics
      where the sky
      falls gray on
      the scattered
           boulders
      false caribou
      antlers under
      the cliffs

      the mountains
      through a fog

May 12, 1977

Sleep

the old man
had to be a
connoisseur

or maybe he
never tried

those women
white wines

the emptied
bottles all
in a row on
the vacated
shelves un-
der his bed

November 24, 1976

Claque

the curtains
close on the
garden scene

one hand too
many in this
hall of mir-
rors and its
silence is a
shadow over-
whelming all
the applause

snagging the
hedges and a
wedge of the
pergola wall

April 18, 1977

Galleries

just once the
taste of what
vanishes sits
on the tongue

the paintings

red pineapple
blankets over
a ruined wall

half the moon
in yellow sky

reproduce all
or nothing of
my properties

I sound these
nearly vacant
corridors for
a new opening

and come upon
one last tomb
which has the
taste of bone

April 4, 1977

Orient

    the outline that comes close to being
less than a face bent sticks pushed a
fathom below water to write the sands

                nothingmoved
                yet it wasn't
                a painting or
                a mirror they
                had shattered
                and carted a-
                way in minia-
                ture cabinets

    one last reflection in the sky
dead ocean without silhouettes

July 7, 1976

At Twilight

straw bristling
out of his neck
the aged farmer

scarecrow for all
occasions without
room to perch
a sparrow
on his shoulder
between flannel
and suspender

as he crept
through
the foliage

February 1, 1977

Celles

fingers opened

chineseshadows
swimming on an
empty wall the
hands float in
milky pools of
lightretracing
pyramids

to make a pair
of gaping lips

angelfish thin
pocket-watches
escape

November 12, 1976

The Exhibit

under the belljar

a soapdish on the
table where it is
close to death at
the far end of an
abandoned bedroom

the last floor if
you go slowly you
can hear its beak
scratching at the
fogged-up glass

October 24, 1976

Chamber Music

   the quartet sometimes
played in the afternoon

brittle leaves
through a window
shadows of bowstrings
   fell between the sun

 and shadows of falling
leaves across the floor
were moving
other silent
     players

March 30, 1977

Natural Gas

the looping
encloses an
other roomy
cell within
a staircase

traces as a
song has it

a cigarette
which bares
no lipstick

metal heels
where a tap
dancer sits
in the dark
waiting for
an elephant
to make her

December 8, 1976

Neglect

    fanning out between
    clover
              bindweed
    the oblong rocks
    calcify
              graywhite
    pigeon specks
               a crust
          rust-colored
        gilding
    where the lichens
    flake off
              smooth
        facets by deep
        crevasses
    crags sprout
    beards of spindly
              moss
    make from a small
    distance the head
    of a dying
        man

February 7, 1977

Traveler

evidence
in a map
of the o
cean

encrusta
tions of
gold and
copper

overland
a web of
tracks I
carry in
the dust

my skull
is empty

December 8, 1976

Portraits

the false
breathing

minute by
minute of
all these
mutilated
paintings

of a dark
forest no
longer in
the walls

a pile of
frames be
neath the
bedspread
empty mir
rors turn
forgotten

glass and
silvering
into dust

May 5, 1977

Pelican Test

the floors uncovered
your palace at night

machine keys turning
the mechanical mouse
360° in the darkness

you can find it when
you put your hand to
the door at the edge
of a faint gleam the
butler tries to hide
in his shallow palms

October 19, 1976

Kestrels

       hedges so high
they leave no room
for anything above
the maze the house
with its kitchen
window lost
            sky no
more than a blot
of fluttering cel-
lulose wings
smokestained wind-
hovers through the
       clouds of
gold church window
saints framed
       in lead

March 23, 1977

Bureauc Rat

sun comes down
little orange pools
   speckle the rug
       redden
disappear

they put another
wall up overnight a
  blind partition
and I am lost

teeth chattering in
a scratchless place

August 10, 1976

Book Worm

moving shadow and perfume
from a gap in the books I
search for the last faces

over gold-stamped leather
spines pages that flake a
wormy snowpath on the rug

one face left for imprint
at the end of the library

navigations and they shut
off the fluorescent light

September 28, 1976

Container

clock ticks
unwinding a
copper coil

taken apart
without the
key

less weight
at midnight
to this box
than to the
obolus full
of sand

March 15, 1977

The Other Frankenstein

    scoria brings in a
nostalgia for infinite
corridors of judgement

he took his reading at
dusk by an open window
from a white substance
beading into pearls at
the bottom of a silver
      bowl

the nude woman walks
where the walls hidden
under a thicket of ivy
and coiling snakes are
hung with poison masks

dead flies drop out of
  her open mouth

October 4, 1976

Batik

mouth black in
a closing cir-
cle   grains
of sand float-
ing dust   the
lips no longer
faded imprints
in the wax un-
less you go on
falling   an-
other way down
white mouth in
a pale cluster
of yellow nets

July 9, 1976

Collector

bluewater ris
ing under the
muddywindows

we keep these
bloated faces
halfsubmerged
in marble

in the cellar
heads with no
imagination

listening for
an earthquake

September 10, 1976

Nostalgia

the times are
passed when a
duchess could
walk with the
tip of a long
cane balanced
on the bridge
of her nose

come to close
the window an
archer lies a
sleep beneath
the tiles

December 17, 1976

Scene of the Crime

upstairs where they keep
the fishheads mounted on
redwood plaques to cover
bloodstains in the wall-
paper someone snuffs the
candle out with his hand

she was breathing faint-
ly in a rocker under the
window listening for his
footfall on the stairs

waiting to open her eyes

September 19, 1976

Omicron

tissue floating a
bove the decimals
driven into these
frozen cobbles by
an icy draft from
a door creaking o
pen at the top of
the staircase

a piece of hatbox

when the god came
out of a house on
the stroke of mid
night wearing his
familiar disguise

October 26, 1976

Recluse

the unfixed space
within four walls
a ceiling and the
floor of semiliq-
uid earth

into which he of-
ten sank his fin-
ger

the abode pleased
him well he could
put up with worms
or maggots in his
dinner as long as
the rent remained
forgotten

he'd taken a room
under the botani-
cal gardens

December 6, 1976

The Webs

with the
twilight
his hot-
air bal-
loons go
up above
the crab
shanties
from the
opposite
shore an
old wom-
an drops
her head
in a box
and says
farewell
to grief

November 8, 1976

Of Mutes

       collecting the spots
       each night
            at the bottom
       of the lampposts she
       crawled out into the
       street from her ram-
       shackle lodgings
            a blue penny
       between her teeth to
       make it easier so
       she wouldn't have to
         swallow her tongue
            and feign
       an epileptic seizure
       if one of the strol-
       lers interrupted his
       nocturnal pantomimes
       to make a sign as if
       to ask her what
         she was about

May 24, 1977

Idiotics

o! those near
or faraway de
scriptions of
an Orient are
raising their
Alhambras be-
fore my eyes!
carry your ey
e in an eyecu
p   a sil
houette had e
azed her coat
less to Hawai
i than an old
crow to a bee
cephalic yule

July 23, 1976

The Search for Napoleon

all the way out to the end of the tiles
you could almost feel the grass growing

when it begins to get dark and the moon
disappears behind a cloud his head pops
up between your swollen feet at the end
of a wheezing bellows you recognize the
Emperor

December 5, 1976

Renard

the last
  with this dis
  solving map in
  the garden
  shadows no
geometer's rings
on the pool
      a fox
between the lily
pads stitches
its eyelids
shut with
    chickenwire

February 11, 1977

Ennui

the door of the
last house when
he knocked fell
open without so
much as a creak

because he took
himself for the
one most likely
to survive when
the storm cloud
had passed over

the old stereo-
scope was lying
on a table made
of polished oak

he put it up to
his eyes by the
blue flame of a
gas-jet and saw

nothing but the
empty street on
a dull winter's
night after the
snow had fallen

November 28, 1976

Mnemes

echo by echo until
the survivors came
to light again the
negative images of
mudhuts and rivers

when the war ended
there were no more
silhouettes in the
hidingplaces under
ground where water
seeped between the
moss-covered rocks
one drop at a time
echo by echo until

October 5, 1976

Plankton

rapture of the not-so-deep
the failing sunlight comes
down greened by the top of
the water   cooled
hypnotic undulations drift
off with the invisible and
the near-invisible   dead
ship gone to the bottom at
the end of its masts hull-
up to be a lost marker below these phantom microbes
nothing moves that isn't a
plant or some kind of fish
that watches shadows swarm
on a sky of glaucous water

July 16, 1976

O

à Pauline Réage

cracks between the rain
swept cobblestones owls
flooding the gutters in
the courtyard of an old
château

I am an owl
under the autumn leaves
wet yellowbrown and red
with a bulging veinwork
between my eyes and the
grating of an oubliette
I look down on you from
above

and you look back at me
under the whip a shadow
two bloodshot eyes from
mingling odors of sweat
leather and mildew swal
low the rest which is a
fleshy mask

October 21, 1976

The Benediction

    if it's here
    the steps going up
    this echo of steps coming down
        through the choir screen
            false tendrils
    old iron branches
    and corrugated hollows
    sound tinted light into tapers
        of smoke and candlewax
    and violins
    cross whispering voices in the
            dark
    if it's here or elsewhere
    you've reached almost the last
    shadow chill of the fresco eye
    that follows you from behind a
        plaster "cloud"

June 18, 1976

Last Kinetoscope

movable slides for nothing
further remains of ears
                gums
  and what passes now
  for the liver
  but laminated
  faces I would
  never be able
  to recall oth
  erwise even a
  set of eyes I
  would like to
lose at the
bottom of a
lake I peer up through the
flickering stench of death

August 16, 1976

Drunk

    how do we resolve
    the underwater madness?
       teacups under plump-
       cheeked tomato faces
       dripping juice

       and oval seeds
       in the carpet-
           pile

    faces I remember
    toads of long ago
    who once leaped out
    of the woods and settle
        now in our cups

May 19, 1977

Impression

gnats flew
around his
empty head

to restore
the invis-
ible order

at the end
of the day
each tooth

bit into a
false rab-
bet of air

to wipe a-
way traces
of a black

meandering
cobweb un-
der an eye

                the lashes
                dropped on
                his window

December 15, 1976

Nightschool

they lit up the room with
plaster faces hung in the
windows   odd
empty heads and a void of
orange rind shredded into
hempstring clots   dead
skin of the catacombs be-
hind their pumpkin "eyes"
•
phrenological curiosities
•
the shellwork alcoves
subtle beats of light

July 22, 1976

Vigil

canyons ranged
in battlements
of eroded rock

we watched the
divers sink in
upright stages
toward a death

sandstone into
limestone took
the full meas-
ure of dawn as
day eroded the
night

August 4, 1976

Legend

purple clouds across the
face of the harvest moon

with the north wind came
the odor of animal pelts
and the track of hunters

branches shook black sil
houettes in the twilight

out where the leaves are
piled for burning an old
hound was tied to a tree
at the edge of the woods

October 27, 1976

Orb

another hunter came
in the night to
scribble his
name on the
wall by
lantern
light
his
face
was nearly
orange but
then a hand came
down on the flaming
             lamp
which made his face
and everything that
once appeared as an
undulating backdrop
painted for a comic
opera sky trees and
the earth vanish to a

December 8, 1976

Properties

each time he
went down to
the basement
he found an-
other alcove
with a trunk

he attempted
to pick each
of the locks
without suc-
cess

later a flea
who had been
rummaging in
a crawlspace
by the mold-
ering stairs
emerged from
a shadow and
murmured

*my trunk
sir have you
seen it any-
where about?*

November 3, 1976

Blue Heron Inn

for Daniel Setzer

the prince of the ruined tower
checked in last night with his
overstuffed valise

I showed him to the room above
my own and so he wouldn't feel
too ill-at-ease we
passed the evening
in a game of
double solitaire

I with my marbles or pegs on a
board pitted with hollows made
of tortoiseshell

he with his dogeared books and
a musty deck of cards on a bed
in the room above mine

December 5, 1976

Toe to Toe

for John Arbelada

she looks away

two eyes above
an empty vodka
glass the café
seems deserted

enter a drowsy
taxidermist to
take her pulse

to tuck in the
telltale wisps
of papersnakes

excelsior from
the breasts to
the thighs you
could strike a
match and burn
the place down

          he strolls off
          under the lamp
          posts with his
          pocket full of
             stuffing

October 15, 1976

Romantic Opium

for Jim Zgorski

taken down under
the pavingstones
to another night
stars pour forth
weak silvertints
our faces coming
up again through
frozen music and
the intersticing
cracks of ice no
closing eye how-
ever black would
ever turn toward
the rising ceil-
ing   alone
I hear the smoke
breakthrough the
ice above an ar-
mature of rusted
sand to melt the
nose of one more

sphinx without a
bottom where the
ice used to be a
cubicle of masks

September 5, 1976

Cinema

for Mike O'Neill

at bottom in
the bloodhut
they let the
film unravel
jerky images

perforations
slightly out
of alignment
made the man
in black-and
-white stum-
ble down the
same rickety
stairs again
without ever
bothering to
look back no
he just went
farther down
beyond reach
of the light

his footfall
in the night
close behind
that door he
will open it

will come in
without even
so much as a
word to take
a seat among
them to wait
in hope that
the next man
halfway down

empty stairs

will sudden-
ly turn back

Friday ?❦ August 13, 1976

Hypnotics

it's almost like being at the shooting-gallery hoping for a tin bear's silhouette to glide by you sit in the dark on a squeaky bed before an open doorway   you hear water running in a bathtub   to get this far you take the backstairs walk the dim labyrinth of corridors over threadbare antique rugs in and out of the lightpools cast down by dusty chandeliers pass through dreary alcoves old Rubens ladies going yellow to their baths behind the granite vases and crumbling statuary urns full of dead twigs no one comes to water   then cracks where pieces of tile have chipped away the blackened space lined with moss green islands in the mud below the final landing turn the key the latch springs back into the room again shoeless into the dark   from the bed you see her through a doorway dressed in her robe going to turn off the bath   the noise of running water dribbles away as she passes by again you hear the dripdrop of a leaky faucet no urns or painted statuary gray like the walls the empty basin and what you see reflected in the mirror the long silence as she walks naked to the tub

July 12, 1976

Germination

    even in this light where
everything loses color a
hair throws long shadows
down the flesh that pass
for other hairs
               below
the belly of this sleep-
ing woman the blond tuft
sinks and rises atop its
double mound
           all that
she loses to the dark in
shape and tint she makes
up for
    what reaches your nose
the lips and the fingers
  what the night reaches
burning deep and immense
under the imaginary hair

August 1, 1976

Man in a Pond

                                              mascara
                              ornamental lashes
                      lipstick and lacquered nails
                          oh those nicotine rings
                            chair denim stains
                            back to the window
she squats
tapping a long jeweled cigarette-holder
pressed through a hole in one of the lower
                                              quarrels
bare rump squashed up the middle hollow
                                to a thick armrest
she watches an old mandarin
lean on his elbow
across the wilted
        hydrangeas
                                  up to his waist
                          between the lily-pads
                 he dares not leave the pond
        but tries every trick in the Book
      of Aquatic Prestidigitation
      to coax her out
                    through the lattice quarrels
                              he can still
                                imagine her
                                    naked

even if she isn't
he wants to have her near him
    clogging about
        a cigarette-holder
      between her painted lips
      sucking the water to trap
      some unsuspecting anchovy
     or blowing bubbles
he'll settle for a little froth
  to get a look at her
     close up
     nude
as he imagines her in hiding
save for a pink cloche hat
so like the tip
of a phallus
    and her black velveteen
        choker

March 20, 1977

Osteology

for Julie Carpenter

through galleries
under muddy skies
the one she found
by a window where
heaps of dirt and
rubble pressed in
on the webcracked
panes had kept on
its mask of bones
and was identical
— as she would be —
to the others who
had felt the bite
of the worm
in search of lost
or long-forgotten
friends

December 12, 1976

Unfinished Diesel

>   dockside
> into the narrows of
> the bay
>   mist
>   where they set us
> afloat on trellised
> winches
>   through ribbons
> of meandering smoke
> we watched the loco
> motive window for a
> sign of life
>
> an oil-stained hand
> behind the throttle
> we abandoned miles
> of untied rails
>   agleam beneath
>   the red-coned
>   fumes of our
>   shunt-lamps

April 14, 1977

Worm Wood

at Witten
berg this
pale-eyed
ghost was
shown old
and dying

Faust now
under the
snows one
evening
had
the Devil
and a lap
dog in to
tea

December 19, 1976

Nautilus

a volute
crushed inside
the fossilized
wall

the ruins
have preserved
one chamber af
ter another of
weblike cities
gone down in a
rubble

one yellow eye
that once swam
over the night
in an ocean of
stars

August 27, 1976

Histories

Rumor

gray sky's archipel

through a window in
the palace of snows
long years planning

underground we took
stairs
    out of an icewall
where the tidalwave
came to be aquarium
glass
    thus they say
the tower was built

March 13, 1977

To Conjure

go back as
far as the
last ditch

she wanted
Solomon to
giver her a
sign

*Kabala und
Liebe* quod
the king

on his
deathbed
a swarm of
devils ap-
peared

November 29, 1976

The Seven Shades

the earth was a lost memory

when the old king died they
buried him under a mound of
anthropological digressions
antique maps and old museum
pieces in yellowed cabinets
the wind or a sudden breeze
    might blow away
his head locked into a but-
    ternut puzzle-box

the dead beasts of the tomb
were seven and made of dust

August 3, 1976

Monody

three sleepless nights
and when I found those
dark dream sites again
the trees were down to
stumps around a ruined
temple in a field like
wooden taborets behind
the creeping buttercup

no priest came to meet
me and of the shadow a
storm cloud hovered on
the blackthorn shiver-
ing to comb a windpath
through the couchgrass
I knew the cobra would
come slithering toward
me fangs opened on the
black sleepless nights
until I found the ruin
again temple and cobra
dark sites of my dream

March 31, 1977

Piscivm

        ocean's last
glitter broken into pools
we return our nets to the
drowned colossus

another moon in fragments
set adrift under the hull
  like so many nightfish
we have sighted land

shimmying through
the veil of water

March 9, 1977

Covered Bridge

    the underwater theatre sinks
    into the lunar depths with
    all its footlights dying

                  no hooves
          clop on the planks
      to find a river underneath

    the wind plays hollow
    on the water no carriage
    lantern swings meandering

March 18, 1977

Luna

black leaves brush
the rooftop of the
abandoned teahouse

the passing clouds

no one will say if
the howl is from a
dog or from a wolf

her eyes conceal a
smile behind white
bridges across the
wind and the night

and she dreams the
face of the hidden
moon

October 8, 1976

Hincha

one song piped through
lianas like strings of
hemp   shaggy green
from the slanting roof
to demon clouds
        broken ripples
in the waters move one
song
     the only boat
                   set
motheaten willow winds
adrift below the porch

suncolored nightingale
in the cage at dusk
   the bars are shadows
over your blinded eyes

February 25, 1977

The Silents

another dynasty

faded landscape
and darkness of
the molehill of
grass where the
Emperor's sleep
sends its fumes
of rot and sad-
ness to us from
one level below

dead until they
buried us eight
maybe nine to a
coffin
 maps rolled up
in velvet-lined
cups to leads us
out of here
            if only we
could find them

May 10, 1977

Soma

downriver out of
grayskies stream
opalescent proto
zoa before a com
ing storm forgot
ten cities piled
under a dripping
screen of nets

goldust minarets
and domes caving
in before an ava
lanche of smoke-
heavy clouds

all the knights-
errant hung rust
ed chain-mail up
to dry in one of
the huts where a
girl was rocking

stroking the cat
with closed eyes

fur like that of
the sphinx

September 16, 1976

Kells

gone then the priest into
his cave to paint our his
tory by torchlight on the
wall of cairngorm

scholar by his cabinet of
bookes head bent low into
the dying light of winter
eld on open pages

for this land that in its
dawning saw the shadow of
Aëlgar's horse extinguish
the sky is fallow

the sword lies broken and
the jackals carry off his
bones traced in dust with
necromantic wands

September 24, 1976

La Complainte Ylvain

for S. Redson

now night has passed
scarlet ribbons into
smoke rises the star
of morning   alone
the succubus left me
here to dream taking
the breath out of my
poor body   ah!
all but the eyes the
ladies hide of their
faces and the veiled
heads that lean over
me!   under
a roof of straw come
shadows where Ylvain
lies full heavy on a
bed of sorrows

Ste Goulache 1976

Hog Tender

on winter days the sun
goes down early behind
the barn a blue shadow
covers the field where
the plow remains a sil
houette two handlebars
and a leather strap on
the clouds at twilight

knee-deep in the slops
where hay is scattered
on a compound of slime
and ooze they speak to
me in squeals of times
long past and grunt of
wanton women that come
to them in dreams like
ghostly apparitions in
the fog they beg to be
remembered not as pigs
    but as forgotten
        sinners

November 11, 1976

Artisan

it rained a long time
to make these mirrors

the sky was black and
mud flowed out of the
ditches sundering the
house where all of us
my wife my cross-eyed
daughter and my idiot
son have lived in the
silence speaking lit-
tle to one another or
never speaking at all

when the rain stops I
will kneel before the
holy place in suppli-
cation to the god for
a moment without wind
that I might look up-
on an unblemished im-
age and know the per-
fection of my work in
water

August 5, 1976

Dante to Enamel

Wenceslaus one frozen morning
the air came out of his mouth
like smoke above the huts before light came he was riding

the foam made icy droplets on
the muzzle of his horse and a
branch fell from an oak broke
like a chandelier on his head

every day was the same as the
day before he would come to a
tree across the boreal wastes
his horse would crumble under
him shattering like an enamel
cask only to reappear when he
returned to the camp alone at
dusk in despair over his lost
kingdom

November 9, 1976

The Plague

under heaven and the
bells or so it seems
the autumn wind blew
full deep across the
druid stones a mourn
ful yule come to the
rusting of each leaf

then where the trees
were bare-dead black
branches on a sky of
lead we carried them
in grave processions
all by wood encoffin
ed to the bone-yards

September 22, 1976

The Conqueror's Horse

when the last of the pine
trees fell apart its dead
needles covered the path-
way back through the wood
and rusted hulks of armor
that lay strewn about the
ground like so many empty
shells the wind played in
after the battle was lost

alone it could almost see
the gutted window pouring
dense clouds of smoke out
of a blackened grotto and
ashes rising to choke the
birds in their nest above
the rocks where the vines
caught fire

December 19, 1976

Chivalric Legend

Messire Hubert
found his love
under ground
in her vault

the veil
put over dying
sparks above a
Syrian graveyard

the last drop is
adamantine night
blood from a cup
rolled along the
parched earth to
an open cemetery

gates where mist
streams in smoke
over the weed to
the headstones

February 21, 1977

Merlin

behind the
eucalyptus
glass par-
titions he
recognized
the voices

made out a
silhouette

the viscid
ripples of
a lost one
in the oil

November 7, 1976

Guelphs

a high-backed chair
engulfed the sun by
a Ghibelline window

Don Alfonso entered
the library wrapped
in his conspirator-
ial cloak and lit a
candle to push back
the gathering shad-
ows

he drew a dagger in
the air as a number
of chairs slid men-
acingly towards him
and vainly tried to
prolong the eclipse

the kingdom of dust
was at hand

December 14, 1976

The Recompense

he climbed the stairs
that made an end to a
dark wood

the room where she
was lying naked under
the canopy of glitter
ing goatfish scales

because he remembered
that once long ago he
had wed the blue-eyed
dame of all his sleep
less nights

October 3, 1976

Astrolabe

        stars resemble
hollow
copper moons
up close they light
        the night

clouds drift
black silver-rimmed
   the smoke across
      their faces

time marks
the wall within
these walls turning
their compasswheels
     to the silent
       navigations
of eternity

February 10, 1977

Watchman

from here the day breaks
under clouds in tints of
emerald green and violet

you're still floating on
the lake in a xebec made
of hollow logs with your
back turned to the moon-
light and the sails down

under the mosquitonet on
your bed in the Caliph's
palace of the clouds you
dream of me the watchman

your hair streaming over
the moveless waters like
some monster of the deep

October 1, 1976

The Moorish Horse

blind eunuchs Nubians
with dirhems fixed to
gilded scales for eye
lids stood watch over
the bath of Yeddahzim
the Sultan's favorite

bluewater covered her
from chin to foot the
depths of the pool un
der the damask canopy
turned her flesh into
eddies of pale marble

the echo went unheard
a tinkling of anklets
struck by the crimson
sun through a colored
window behind the bil
lowing muslin curtain

it came dark nostrils
sniffing the scent of
burning ambergris and

foam flecks lathering
its muzzle the eye in
a circle of wet ashes

October 14, 1976

The Assassins

came night we clothed ourselves
in animal skins and walked amid
the severed heads on pikes like
mute ghosts where the earth ran
dark with the blood of two dead
armies

we had taken the mountains down
piece by piece cutting deep into the granite walls which made
an ancient pyramid when all the
soil and grass fell into debris

and we could not find the place
of entry

October 10, 1976

Peregrination

cribblings on the
palm or in a pool
below the terrace

the map comes too
near the crossing
of words to be an
effigy of our un-
known geographers

sand scatters its
traces in number-
less variegations
under the caravan
wheel

April 13, 1977

Carnaval Ending

    the adept
    cautioned
        "know the *finis* that
    comes soon after the fall
    of the last card
      in Venice you will find
      no gondolas to take you
    upriver
        the old carriages tip
      their broken axletrees
    toward muddy canal waters
    where nothing can breathe
    when this *faro* game is
    done"
        dawn light covers
      the old basilisk under
    a heap of glittering dung
    barnacles

March 27, 1977

Winter

    mottled twilight falls
    —houses
        sinking under
            chimneysmoke—
  on the drowning horses

none without this
ice to put them to sleep
in the distance would be
  recognizable from here

sunspots through
tines of freezing water

"what do you want then?"

          to come as far
as the river would allow
behind these white dunes
until night holds back
the stench of their
burning carcasses

January 30, 1977

Obeah

when he had snuffed out
the last of the candles
with a moistened finger
and thumb he groped for
other methods of illumi
nation   the mirror
in a top dresser drawer
kept one white image un
der a dust of centuries
she was unremembered in
the dark she opened her
eyes and she almost saw
him waiting for a green
spark to light her face
to cast a shadow on the
stars

October 28, 1976

Amnesia

he would make his coffin as large as a warehouse strung from end to end with piano-wire   it suited his tastes to begin the excavations at nightfall close by the edge of the sea   he made tentative soundings of unsoundable mud with an ear to the ground and picked at the ashes between his teeth   reeds murmured as he dragged them up out of the dunes he forgot that he had planned another death in the same way and one before it and still another more rudimentary on a treadmill lined with padded silk while like a hard-boiled egg out of its shell his lifeless remains passed in waferthin slices through the rusty strings of an old harp

July 29, 1976

Bivouac

after the evening meal
he could hear the peal
of the seagull echoing
across the dunes as he
flicked the crumbs off
the tablecloth and un-
rolled the map

"gentlemen" he said in
a hushed tone of voice
placing his snifter on
one of its yellow cor-
ners for a weight "the
undiscovered city"

October 25, 1976

Crawl Space

they were lying side by
side mouths open in the
mud gas-bloated bellies
faces black from powder
burns blind eyes rolled
back toward heaven with
smoke pluming up out of
their open wounds after
the battle was lost

someone found the open-
ing under a trench with
the remains of his hand

poked through the clots
to what was left of his
skull behind the spider
web

September 29, 1976

Quadrant

however far we get
one deep pie slice
of murk follows us
out from this land
across the eternal
wastes

what never changes
is a room and what
one sees through a
window

the waters move an
unknown provenance
under the stars at
dusk to lead us in

small patches rust
a faint pox on the
bleeding-glass

April 3, 1977

The Captive

behind red maples
the weeds shadows
in the late after
noon across stone
walls

this cell is cool
enough and almost
as dark under the
barred windows as
it is by the door

they pass my food
to me on a silver
plate

I will stay again
tonight

one could not eat
half so well as
this on the
outside

November 17, 1976

Herbal

for bleary eyes *angelica*

the beggar
ticks hide their baskets
in the cleft of the rock
or tie their money up in
cords of whitened sorrel
to keep the gods in envy
of their secret riches

smooth tracks on the
beach at night after the
tide recedes

for the sorrow *monkshood*

the sorrow of their gods
who knock at our bedroom
windows pleading to know
what has become of their
ancient powers

April 6, 1977

Occasions

Arcology

for Angelo

the order of the words
made little difference
to him now

his survey of Algerian
pissoirs recalled some
final excavation

years spent in the un-
known cities he had no
time to remember

Labor Day 1976

Phantom

without the words
I come to watch a
swarm of protozoa
nebulæ transpar-
ent filaments and
white tracks in a
drift of snow the
pieces soundless-
ly float under my
rheumy eye across
an empty sheet of
paper

Guy Fawkes Day 1976

October Nights

    long ago the ocean
    heaved and covered
    the stars with the
    shadows of ancient
        monsters

    two legless horses
    still rock by moon
    light teetering in
    the falling leaves

    one with a sparrow
    in its teeth wings
    fluttering up into
        a tree

    one that waits for
    me gills breathing
    with the hiss of a
    bellows at the end
      of my yard

Halloween 1976

Elevations

she sees him again one
can be no quicker than
the hand however quick

what he was before the
snowy morning in a mir
ror with his head chop
ped off he's no longer
the eye of a needle if
a camel wishes to pass

through his glittering
iris to the other side

Mort du Père Ubu 1976

The Shore

the ocean empties its masks

on the beach the sand takes
form in a hardening cast of
jellyfish glaucous anemones
white bones

what's left
of the wreckage long before
twilight is picked clean by
the jackals

scattered in the four winds

All Souls' 1976

Expectation

for six months
only dark through
    the winter here

now that has
        lessened

we take
our time about it
    nonetheless
though they wait
where light will
        be
the cold steam of
breath vaporing
their faces
    for us
to come out

Groundhog Day 1977

Apparatus

he used to tuck the
heart in transverse
slices behind these
tumbledown walls

    to show the rind
or these membranous
innards to the best
advantage

           pickled
in lieu of a window
in a bottle of wine

St. Valentine's Day 1977

Lent

        glass of bock
    three-quarters drained
    on the table marbling

            ochre lace
      for window-curtains
      put a thin moss on the
      dark brew

           beads foam
      half a finger's depth
      above the dregs
      I won't give up

Ash Wednesday 1977

A Rheum for the Night

beyond all claustrophobic fumigations

empty furniture and the ticking of an
unencumbered timepiece the whispering
four women betray in my bed framed by
the balcony window with a new moon in
the cloud behind their smiling phases

April Fools' Day 1977

The Dead Fish

1

wood
near to rotting
away all of a
midsummer's
night
for
opalescent
scales glitter-
ing there under
a stunted tree
outside of our
moonlit bar-
racks

2

and never we
forgot that oily
savor of it
in the pan
long
it lingered even
after the eyes

fell out of it
like a pair of
acid coins
rolling to
the weeds

Holy Week 1977

MEMOIRS

Protozoa

gray in the cloud
I'm writing again
to see the specks

wingflutters like
blank letterpaper
disappear insects

faint butterflies

the days too long
nights too silent
and a carbon lamp
to light the beds

October 18, 1976

Red Weather

early one October morning
after the rain fell and a
puddle under the door had
frozen into a pond of ice
over the blue-green tiles
of Mrs. Jatzeva's kitchen
we sat at breakfast wait-
ing for the bread to thaw
and witnessed by accident
the Second Coming

it was done with a set of
tiny "mirrors" old razor-
blades a family cockroach
who had nothing better to
do with himself once used
as a pair of skates

Old Taupman sitting on my
left passed me the butter
and suddenly came to life
mumbling through his gums
that even in the Dark War
which he alone remembered

when the trenches ran red
when extraordinary things
were the order of the day
he had seen nothing to e-
qual this

October 20, 1976

My Room at 8 O'Clock

black stairways crossing
in and out of shadows on
their way to nowhere un-
der   above
and below a dizziness in
graywhite space dark ru-
mors suspended above no-
thing below nothing four
figures teetering by the
heavy ropes where splin-
tered ends of the
            catwalks
      try to meet at
dusk   warp
and woof of the curtains
to mottle what's left of
a slanting twilight over
one of Piranesi's
       prisons

July 9, 1976

Cricketing

tracks paper the wall
with ashes
I can sketch her face
 and still remember
all the hidden noises
by rubbing her ankles
 together
*
the bones
are all I
have left
of my old
unpapered
room
*
this room has the woman
still reasonably intact

July 8, 1976

Cuckold

I married
the woman
connected
by dotted
    lines

she wants
a divorce

I'll have
to use my
eraser on
her mouth
   and
   below
 to keep
 the peace

or pay it
off in al
  imony

December 8, 1976

Jorgue

my brother:
an odd case

red goggles
tied around
his leather
pilot's cap
he sets his
plants in a
potted cir-
cle without
remembering
to move the
scatter-rug

he wants to
cut a round
spy-hole in
the ceiling
just to let
in the rain

we push his
lunch under

the bedroom
door but he
has no more
time to eat

August 2, 1976

Pairs

they take you into a domed room
a huge amphitheatre in the dark

you can just make out a console
green-glass keys reflections in

a blackness without contours of
faces lost in the bottom shadow

October 12, 1976

Clockwork

a woman in the window
that night we went to
repair the old grand-
father clock she came
as far as the landing

in platform heels and
gartered stockings so
transparent you would
never have known they
were there in the dim
light of Mrs. Pittz's
vestibule

we try not to pay at-
tention
      the work is hard
and naked women are
distracting

May 16, 1977

Outside a Library

       mid-winter
       in the sky
       pale bi-focals
       after the snows
       twin suns head on
       late in the after
               noon
       and no gray
       clouds were left
       footbridge planks
       under an old tree
              maple
      across the wood
       have melted
         creak

February 15, 1977

In the Hôtel Orfila

lamplight and shadows
melting in an unremem
bered weave of velvet
or threadbare brocade
made vague landscapes
writhe in a room with
out windows

the chairs are not as
deep as they were the
night I first came to
sleep at the Hôtel no
one asked me if I had
need of a bed

December 16, 1976

Polydor in Bed

with the window blinds
left open at night the
gray light of a porch-
lamp cast long shadows
from across the street

a slow dissolve toward
the pitch black mirror

he came to see himself
floating on his back a
few inches off the bed
given up to a darkness
without depth contours
or color he started to
cry out after this im-
age which was about to
become an unsculptured
mass of specks

November 23, 1976

Dead Letter

bone-marrow and
teeth sent with
no return
address

the everpresent
silhouettes

another airmail
envelop of dust
she opened once
without reading
between the
lines

December 1, 1976

Rorschach

shriveled leaf-marcescing trace
of watery brown on yellow paper
made the devil-bat with pointed
ears blank oblong snout and the
crab-shell held together by two
broken ribs one at the neck the
other crossing the belly as a ʌ

which without a head might be a
walrusmustache or the cutaneous
lips guardian beauties of Vulva
where the pages join 114 to 115

the chapter on algæ in Nightin
gale's *Text-Book of Botany* 1906

August 31, 1976

Eclipse

she turned
beyond the
trees open
doors into
a footpath
muffled in
the rug we
caught her
underneath

a greenish
sky tipped
into black
up against
the window

faces van-
ishing un-
der a van-
ished moon

August 12, 1976

Aftermath

he opened the
windowseat to
fool the cook

took one step
down into the
hidden depths
of the secret
cupboard this
room disturbs
me nothing is
in its proper
place back up
the stairs he
is singing in
another voice

she hears him
from the cup-
board-window-
seat but can-
not recognize
the olde tune

August 25, 1976

Sideshow

he went behind
the curtain to
have a look at
all the freaks
belles petites
pin-head women
Orientals what
could spit al-
most a quarter
mile through a
sky-light win-
dow with their
nostrils if no
one was around
they dozed off
under the tent
dreaming while
he conducted a
rehearsal from
a nearby alley
alone with the
pantomime rats

July 19, 1976

Sadness

we often encouraged
him to leave his
bed if only for the
turbulence of mists
and gathering water
    on the wall
pieces without dawn
tea-rose geometries
he had to close his
eyes to every morn-
ing
subtle replications
beneath unlaundered
    hospital sheets
to which he had be-
come the Galileo of
an inner darkness
  he wanted nothing
more than to forget

August 28, 1976

Tango Mask

he envisaged a white
face
         old motets
of velvet smudged in
red he had later use
for pickling
         two eyehole-
gaps of escape to
the nostrils and the
interstices of their
lips
         to scribble
obscene messages on
the executive wash-
room mirror
an island lost
where they both dis-
robed two puppets on
the end of an umbil-
icus
their eyes rolled in
wooden sockets under
         the lunar crust

August 15, 1976

Water Mark

    with a mixture
    of what lies in
        the background
            for color

    the pool spreads a
    liquid skin skimming
    the porcelain hollow
        with the stopper
            plugged in

        the center
        of a froth
        of bubbles

        silverthread
    the faucet spews out
    of its muzzle a hair
        thin cylindrical
            mirror

February 4, 1977

Modifications

for all these
heads no long
er in use the
chamber below
stairs was an
unknown haven
built to mask
their all too
fleeting memo
ries of a sep
aration

a place where
objects which
could be seen
only from the
neck down
were kept

November 30, 1976

Feeding

mouth amid counters o-
verflowing with bric-a
-brac

    center-
darkness in a fluores-
cing vignette unencum-
bered gums into a ton-
sil quivering with ex-
pectation

neither man nor beast-
ly unicorn it was pos-
sessed of neither head
nor trunk nor extremi-
ties

the proprietor fed his
pets every day at this
time without regard to
species

August 11, 1976

Reliquary

without
the smoking tapers
or the censer fumes
curling against the
top of the vault to
 make the limestone
   blacker yet
they could not have
found anything more
in this hand or ear
or splinter of des-
iccated fingernail
than a thimble-cup
to hold the unused
ashes of their
         priest's cig-
              arettes

he liked them
     at breakfast
  to sprinkle over
   his deviled eggs
in lieu of pepper

April 27, 1977

Album

    for this book
    crusted paintflecks
      holes in a screen
        with your face
          behind it
(a dream) blotted
            out
all of a piece
the eye
          an ear
    red-golden fuzz
    against its rim
  to shell the wires
in a passed up sun

for this book
all the more recent
    photographs
  of you

March 17, 1977

Exergue

       something to buy-
       off a judge
           one in three
       verso of the coin
       old parlor magick
       the last within
           and without
       one into an angel
       naked genii
       to the waist with
       ribbed prehensile
       tales to dream on
       tails to set them
       rocking above the
       bottom line
           ancient
       table-leg deities
       come to life in a
       green carpet-pile

May 3, 1977

Apprentice

the faces on these
half-decayed walls

gaping mouths like
tiles of blue moss

he served his time
in the pit scaling
the backs of alli
gators for *coppers*

oxidized coins the
kids tossed from a
high gallery under
the crumbling dome

for the whisperers

May 17, 1977

The Ending

the hiss of
leather tongues to
beat down the weed
brought the nettle
    to blood

the nose
and the corners of
lips when again we
  reached the place

to get there
we cut a wide path
through the avenue
of crumbling wall –
    nut trees
past hedges
of murderers' moss
until the sun came
  to water our eyes

May 15, 1977

Crevass

    symmetries masked
    along the defile
            mystery
       of lost faces
    and no one looked
    back
         to the ledge
    crumbling pebbles
    into the widening
    gulf of ice
        of music boxes
    chiming sad tunes
    in a dusty room

April 19, 1977

Bal

another sound

I hear a mask
rustle   the
one thing you
still have on

a nude silhou
ette within a
downy halo of
peach-fuzz to
set your body
in an eclipse

December 7, 1976

Repository

high window lookout
letting a gray light
   in through the bars

lost in an ocean
our keel scraping
off the rooftops of
   a London street
    toward the park
   it might be raining
still
will they never come
again to claim their
baggage?

     a ray of dust on
trunks and old foot-
lockers by the grimy
wall soon to be
submerged

February 3, 1977

Eaters

those of the attic

peach trees leaning out of
the loft

who watched in silence the
margin of swarming insects

—the dilapidated roofs
of our abandoned factories
far from what was once
the street became a
woods where crab-
grass crept into
the eaves—

had come too near the edge
of these hollow debris
to turn back

April 11, 1977

Arrival

the conductor was
already too drunk
to be dreaming it

close to midnight
with leaves brush
ing at the window
we felt the sleep
ing-car lurch

we tumbled out of
our bunks and the
train pulled into
a tunnel of owls'
nests

September 27, 1976

Women

      one I seem to recognize
      steps out from the mass
      of steamy flesh
         and walks toward me

      women
      they go under
      a cloud of nets
      and never look back
      across the beaded tiles

      long yawning spaces en-
      veloped the distance in
      fog
              train windows
          full of anxious faces

March 16, 1977

Haunted

I did not recognize
them when they came
to me on the nights
of the quarter moon

other nights I shut
my eyes and ears to
their noise and let
them babble on till
they grew bored

their heads were un
der black hoods and
they spoke to me in
muted cries or else
in whispers

November 14, 1976

Trist

the heart
I vaguely
come back
to in the
lumberous
corridors

just this
side of a
last beat

predatory
orbs that
gaze over
my shoul-
ders as I
creep to-
ward your
dormitory
bed

Vanessa

May 23, 1977

Possessions

there's nothing
left of the old
house but these
stones that she
keeps locked in
a bureau drawer

behind the mat-
tress where the
wall used to be

the dead leaves
she stuffed her
pockets with at
night to make a
mask are out of
reach

December 6, 1976

Erasure

the sun came up
in a dusty wind
behind a web of
old spiderglass
halftransparent
insects crawled
on spindle legs
through shadows
thin veins in a
blind man's eye

he did not stop
to put out what
was left of the
redflame in his
jack-o'-lantern

October 11, 1976

Decor

a few
black lines
were needed
to make the
window come
right

faces
singed with
monkey dust
took him as
far as this
chair

where
he will sit
letting the
new tenants
rock him to
sleep

until
the cobwebs

gather in a
dark corner
of the cor-
ridor

April 7, 1977

The Thing

    squat in the dark part
of the hallway I awake to
an aftertaste of the worm
termite dozing underneath
my tongue with folded
wings to relieve
itself
        of another letter
  the way it first came to
me so thin that I needed
the butter knife
to let it out

April 12, 1977

Pluvians

no one can see
our rooftops
    from here
    the puddles
stir their mud
and we plummet
out of sight
behind a cloud
    our windows
lost in a silt
so deep it can
have no bottom
under the rain

May 25, 1977

Aphid

he seldom spoke and
no one ever saw him
at the evening meal

often in the middle
of the night waking
in a sweat from his
recurring dream un-
der the sooted hot-
house windows where
he found himself in
costume drawing the
sap out of a cring-
ing plant stem with
his hairy snout the
old tenant was at a
loss for what to do

the new tenant kept
his pair of goggles
in a dresser drawer
by day under cello-
phane wings

November 22, 1976

After the Journey

so in the end when no
one was around to see
him leave he squatted
on an old slab of tim
ber expecting a tidal
wave to carry him off

out of the winecellar

green bottles covered
in a film of dust all
the way up to the raf
ters which ended in a
stairway the owner of
the house had left un
finished

September 4, 1976

Orcq

I can remember
only fragments
of the telling

grass with the
eyes turned on
a green amœba

underneath the
stories of the
living are how
the living had
come to be the
dead

April 17, 1977

Isle

the cedars go down in
terraces to the walls

images broken in rip-
pling water below re-
flections of slablike
mausoleums the crick-
ets and the ticks are
chewing the wood-lice

when you die they put
you under with a rood
in your hand

August 30, 1976

Gothick Recess

they practiced
their dance on
the narrow-cob
bled alleys at
night beyond a
graveyard wall

from the tombs
you could only
hear them beat
ing their dull
lichen-spotted
wings over the
cemetery slabs

then the clock
chimed echoing
in the dormers
of the rickety
houses calling
them in before
the break of
dawn

May 18, 1977

A General's House

      black was
the night he died
  the General saw
his wife's eye in
the glass the lid
closing and open-
ing a crescent of
lashes underneath
the brandy dregs
  were the locusts
chichering in the
trees outside the
General's granite
mansion removed
      to a final
mask of ink blots
from the blotter
to the lamp

May 26, 1977

The Night Before

the night before the war broke out

extinguished lampposts in the murk
black sails fluttering down across
the windows   we found the door
unlocked and crept in through dark
headways climbing a vestibule wall

the old man was sitting in a chair
trying desperately to rock without
giving a thought to the silhouette
across the matting of dead beetles

he took it for a shadow rocking in
the debris fallen of the night before

March 7, 1977

Specimen Teeth

    they shut up this mansion at
midnight
        tickless
              wanderings
at the top of the stairway a
ghost makes its presence
known as the mistral light
poured out of a crack in
the wall to read
the false meandering
that might be a hair
or the branch of a yew dying
on its tongue the imprints
that never last long
enough to be
recalled
in the morning

March 24, 1977

The Other Voice

hung on the ledge
canvas in tatters
up the moist wall
paper
faint neon lights
outside my window

a wolf speaks
mimicking the old
man's voice

he comes at night
to beg for scraps
of meat

Old Glover at the
wood with his tin
knuckle
knocking the door

March 28, 1977

Portmanteau

with no one to attend him
      he shook again
old rotted maxillæ the clacking teeth of memory strung up by a rope
      heads bloodied the winding-sheet he carried from place to place on the moonlit afternoons he was allowed to go out alone
    the others kept to their rooms — *camera obscura* — projection of a city by the lake upside down on one of the inner walls
      rust-colored hair trailing from lower branches to the grass

May 29, 1977

Sync Dying

breakwater dark inter-
twining nets went par-
achutes after flounder
and belly-up sardines

    straw boaters
in the window falling
leaves the last he was
to see afloat

    downriver willows
front porch scavengers
coral and castaways

    autumn come
the scarecrows walking
straw-foot on the roof
above the room where
    Sync lay dying

March 22, 1977

The Toll

                    alone
              he watched
the ceiling come to mid-
night
                  no wind
         or patter of rain
on the windows
the laths rattled
            to wake him
          one more time
        and no one came
to close his eyes or
take the wet cheesecloth
           from his brow
midnight
he died in the listening
               chamber

February 22, 1977

Numbers

enough time had
elapsed for him
to measure the
fall of
dust
        he went
      upstairs in
    his slippers
a secret rendez
vous to keep be
fore the stairs
lost form under
the gray drifts
he could feel a
hollow opening
    beneath his
        feet
small
cascades of
dust into the
widening trench
that sucked him
down just as he
was about to re

create what lay
behind the last
mask of the end
less masquerade

November 24, 1976

Sundering

we brought them all
the way to the edge
and pushed them off

no one can show you
the ocean dead they
are gone beyond re-
membering with eyes
closed faces turned
to the deep

nothing above
nothing below

black dots plummet-
ed noiselessly into
foamy wreaths

July 28, 1976

Palace of Hong Kong

                    twilight
through grimy windows a
rose corridor where the
women climb nude out of
the marble bathing pool

no other sound than
the print of their feet
on the white and yellow
                        tiles

white and Chinese women
we know by their hair
above and below
                triangles
    the water darkens

wet-heavy dripping mats
they squat to dry
    and powder

May 22, 1977

Cyclostome

from my window

to bring in an
eel or a blind
lamprey called
Vampire of the
Deep in a ship
 wrecked book

the glimmer of
a star between
two clouds the
night is black

but I can hear
you walking on
the pebbles by
the ocean drag
ging your nets

December 13, 1976

Memoirs

         a nap
with the curtains
drawn
   in the dimness
of the ceiling no
shadow crossed to
make the green of
the lawn less
         green
as it filtered in
above the curtain
rods
  those afternoons
when she was gone
or all but gone
coming
     palms open
on this bedspread
where hollows now
flesh-tinted are
  another shade of
green in the murk

February 20, 1977

This Side of the Silence

The Bottom Page

      what he reads
taken up
in mid-sentence
with no inkling
of where or to whom
      it might lead

white distances
impossible to trace
  in the snow or to
  walk over without
    slipping through
    the blue shadows
of drifts when
     under the elms
     the second branch
tumbles in a broken
window far from the
fall of other
     silent trees
  within a room
  he comes to them
  after the house is
gone and only these

pieces of cut glass
remain
        shadowless
letters on the snow

with no inkling
of where or to whom
    they might lead

May 1, 1977

An Imitation Light

    counterfeit distances
    where all depths were
        swallowed in a wall
    of fluttered scaffolds
    piled against the door
    old graveyard cocoons
          made move
      another in what
    darkness knew to be
    short-lived vessels

    souls pumped
    empty of the bloodwind
     gave form to formless
        shadow debris

March 21, 1977

The Synthesis

       absence is
what can never be
effaced from this
room
    even in debris
other shapes take
form but only
      as the city
once took form
       if the eye
or better
       the land
beyond the eye is
there to draw the
marrow out of its
ruins' echoing
      bones

April 28, 1977

The March

    you can go only
    so far
           before
    the river comes
    up black
         a little for
            death
    old buildings
        reduced
        to skeleton
    shadows above a
    mound of broken
    rocks
          cinders
    survivors of an
    entombment

March 8, 1977

Settings

tilting
the solar dish
at sunset half
a shadow and a
little less of
the wire monu-
ment two miles
from the edges
    of eclipse
I turn
the knob again

    sun's gray
ball goes down
the horizon to
a few wan yel-
low candles in
a gable window
far across the
open space

May 11, 1977

Blem

    flame-tongues
    point the way to
               eclipse

    corona

    the split-tipped
    sun is black now
    mountainpeaks in
               gas

    silhouettes
    finger the night

February 13, 1977

Balloon Gondola

   with a sky noise
   pail half full of water
             beneath
   to strike a mimic
   of the sea
        and no balloon
           to bring it
              down

   suddenly years later
   less of what passes for
      clouds to see over
         the absence
            of balloon
   gondola hangs
   from withered cedar
      branches tied to
         tufty rigging
          no more

March 2, 1977

Feline

black diamonds
cover its eyes
after the lamp

vague floaters
of a lost room
in green coals

the soft steps
he cannot hear
across the rug

it alone keeps
the image of a
claw very near

and where this
claw must come
to bury itself

even its ghost
a second after
the lamp

Friday ⇒ May 13, 1977

Orpheus Rocker

for the night is a
corner of the room

the motets of dust
pass in silhouette
through flashes of
what cloisters the
town from my sleep

a screen above the
projected canopies

where the two ends
of the wall come a
long way off to me

April 24, 1977

Recall

goodbye to
the bridge

occasional
diversions

in a green
room where
an actress
wipes away
her makeup

goodbye to
the bridge

in a dusty
mirror the
dark light
bulb burns

November 24, 1976

Before the Switch

>his emptied coffers
>closed blind spaces
>at the rim of night

>pink traced against
>the coming darkness

>near sleep he moved
>pale fingers across
>an edgeless light

March 29, 1977

Cartograph

Celebes or
Borneo the
islands in
an ocean a
black line
makes over

I draw the
reflection

my handles
on the cen
ter depths

October 17, 1976

Rites

    when sun is down
they send the dog
into the conduits
with a flashlight
tied to its neck

    none will ever
find the way home
without the dog's
bark echoing back
to them through a
vague distance of
ribbed metal
and concrete

    the same lost
distance to cover
every night while
they wait for the
end of a silence
that never comes

May 26, 1977

Moon-Blind

floating noiselessly
no other sound where
between gloved wings
above my pate an orb
came fluttering down

to cover up a little
of the moon under my
window I have placed
the last of the dead

gray smiles across a
field of wheatstalks

the crows after dark
shadowing the horses
crack their beaks on
all my hollow skulls

April 20, 1977

Moments

you take them
down with you

    all rooms
    all doors
    no echoes

windows tilt-
ing cloud re-
flections the
sky can never
descend lower

empty columns
dwindled into
a few seconds
of deathsmoke

soundlessness
in mute ticks

August 8, 1976

Exhaustion

at the very end
of this process
there is almost
nothing left to
see

it leans on its
paws and crawls
for water along
the edge of the
rug

not even a room
remains of what
falls under the
eyes in the mir
ror

September 17, 1976

Fireside Audience

from here all I can
see are their round
eyes gleaming above
the logs   pairs
of floating coals a
shade too bright or
flaming traces in a
window   trails
falling through the
night   shadows
behind the curtains

they move noiseless
ly   no one
can hear the sounds
they make to tickle
the fleas and whisk
the cinders off the
chimney bricks they
have come down only
to warm their hands
over the gray ashes

September 21, 1976

Fzzz

here
in a
tank

legs
arms
head
toes
that
cor-
rode
this
acid
bath

drop
away

December 6, 1976

The Box

        he listens
for the cushion to spring
dust and mothballs at him
from the last of his sour
wanderings
        it opens
a wake of oceans obscured
by dark blisters
of twilight
        and whimmers
the face in its setting
disk of blood-red streaks
clouds in the eyes
        nose and mouth
extinguished as far as
his ears where the shower
of black sparks becomes a
deadening pre-echo
        of the night

May 2, 1977

Gemian

when mud fills
the water like
brownish smoke
what swims off
under the dead
eye of a blind
watchman keeps
its fins above
the sanddrifts
a broken cloud
where the suns
go red to meet
the ocean in a
curve of blood

October 29, 1976

Parallels

under the lens granules
in a landscape of slabs
that open the last mile

dunes

with the moon gone down
the ocean turned to ice
cut through rockcrystal
at the bottom of gloomy
craters

sand of the polar night

August 26, 1976

Etiquette

after the dinner was taken away
uneaten
                    he took up
the xylophone kept hidden
under the dining table for such
accidents as might occasion
an insufficiency of cuisine

with an ear to the metal keys
he would listen till the melody
ran on to an ineludible
disintegration
                    unless the tune
was played by another
under the napkin so to speak

in which case all music becomes
equivalent silence

April 4, 1977

Nemesis

    the monkey tottered
near the edge of an
old armoire:
    "I have suffered
eddies of broken
light
        small dents
beneath the windows
too shallow to note
        ormolu
    and traces
of linoleum
    clear droplets'
    foursquare panes
with the whole room
bent out of shape
around them
as in a
lens"

        footprints
    cut a quiet path
through the dust
to where it fell

March 1, 1977

Echo

when there was
no one left to
call he erased

the last trace
of voices echo
on the tapes

an unknown man
or a gnome who
mimics his old
way of talking
says *he cannot
let it end un-
til I can make
sure that when
I die you also
will have lost
everything but
your memory of
this voice
which then
will truely be
my own*

November 14, 1976

The Medium

    where the trees are suddenly
cut down at the verge of the
woods
                clearing
he knew once never to forget
his room was there the doors
the same doors closing again
under a square patch of open
sky
             lit a footpath
through shimmering moth-dust
from the closet threshold to
the gilt-edged claws of this
      old magicians'
        throne

April 25, 1977

Inside

       that moonblot on greenish
       skin the last   black
       quarter bristling over an
       uncut diamond one flaw to
       sleep like a dying animal
       paws in the air under an-
       other moon a cinder ready
       to burn a smoking pinhole
       down through the blue ice
       the second flaw is hollow
       and turns in a vacuum the
       third rattles a merry set
       of bones on the head of a
                        pin

July 13, 1976

An Anecdote

coffee stains on the bark
of this tree and how they
got to be there

an owl up in the branches
settling unfinished moons
in the grass before night
fell pecked for a room in
the trunk hoping that the
right knothole might give
way

in the process of which a
dried puddle crusted with
coffee grounds came close
to being recognized

and would have been if he
had known that coffee was
something not often found
in the barks of trees
or even of dogs
for that matter

May 5, 1977

Doubling

only one way down to
the wine-cellar from
here you lift up the
grating and put your
eye to the dark gulf
inches above the rug

a metal chute echoes
back someone's voice

and from his bed the
other one halfasleep
tries to reconstruct
the room where he is
halfasleep beginning
with the bookshelves

ending in the mirror
with its pictures of
moldering labyrinths
and webconnected bot
tleracks underground

September 23, 1976

Excavation

we brought
up the remains

castle fragments
sketched against the
debris of earthquake

gutted windows where
the sky came down in
blackened pieces the
hulking shroud of an
elegant wolf and old
world-weary mansions
fell like a house of
cards

November 30, 1976

Someone

no the grass is full
of weeds or the roof
slopes down much too
low   a
shadow   a spot of
charcoal and dust if
you sift through the
ashes to rearrange a
leg or turn the head
to one side the nose
crumbles away then a
small portion of the
ribcage like a house
caving in toward the
eyes   deep sock-
ets going deeper in-
to wind   unless

July 15, 1976

Limn

who knows where
to find the edge
     of this?

two of us
left to go on in
    the dark

to try and reach
the door
  only two of us
if
the door is shut

one alone if
the door is open
then I will have
    imagined
  that the one
  who searches
with me now
had not found
the edge as I

         had found it
         if there was
           an edge
          to find

May 4, 1977

Towards Midnight

under the veil
of steam she
finishes

neverchange
the coffee-pot
dread widow
comes

spidermask
wiping her eye
glass having
neither pupil
nor iris

finishes
outlines
traced
across
the blind side
of her

February 7, 1977

Haze Elegy

no balloonwithered
drop-clouds if the
sky is hidden past
smoke into its mel
loworange disk the
tops of trees fade
until there are no
more edges left to
make an end of our
breathing we close
our hands over the
crabgrass and wait
for what's left of
a sun to come down

August 24, 1976

Witness

the lodger had taken a bag of darjeeling tea into the breakfast-room sat down by the coalstove with an empty cup in one hand the tea bag in the other and rocking from side to side took a glance or two around the shadowy corners of the old furniture weatherworn oaks mahoganies and tackstudded velveteens under their antimacassars and a covering of dust you could smell in the air before settling in for his long stare through tinted windows at the dawn

    why do you want to know these things?

he watched the sun come up put the teacup on his head

bit into the gauzy tea bag
and then there was nothing

an orange disk widened behind a fog veined with the
branches of the dead trees

August 29, 1976

Eviction

      alone
in that room above
         the barn
   with nothing to
  light the yellow
papers he had car-
ried this far in a
wheelbarrow up the
  gravel road with
     the last of his
       furniture
hoarfrost fogging
the windows behind
which he was
a dark blur
recalling
other journeys
he had made and
would make again
     by night
    waiting for

someone to knock
at the door
and offer
him
 a book of matches

November 16, 1976

The Baths

bubbles rising to
break the surface
with an acid fizz

only the skeletons
at night to watch
them sink

seldom a watchman

blurred beneath a
ripple of yellow-
ing fixer

the images deepen
in a shallow tray
elements that had
once clung to the
bone are ready to
reassemble a face
sucked dry of all
its blood

a background with
the eyes alone or

glimmers of stars
where red touches
red in the whites
of the eyes

May 9, 1977

Cow Catchers

clouds swell and
blacken near the
railroad tracks

    we stand
under the clouds
with our arms in
plaster casts
hoping that
this time
        it will
  only mean rain

then an udder
protrudes out of
the lowering fog

  and we must
  brace ourselves
for a plummeting
of cows again

May 19, 1977

The Diva

    branches below a
lunar sky
      the copper key
turning the lock

    someone walks in
on tiptoe finger
to lips across a
space of shadows

      I can tell now
from the hiss of
watered-silk old
tunes drift back
to my ears where
she whispers
      suddenly
beside me on the
divan
      so close
to me that I can
almost touch the
sound of her
      voice

May 8, 1977

To the Ruin

                they will come
to search among the rocks for a
sign of what never dies
    amid these fatal imprints
when the old city is demolished

a theatre shut in by the rubble
its curtains torn to shreds and
the upended loges glittering
    jagged slivers of chandeliers
caved in on the ridge overhang-
ing this obscure ravine

        faint silhouettes of men
on horses near the gray horizon
through a shroud of mist

April 22, 1977

Interregnum

something rotted quietly
hulking through the dark
cellar beneath our shoes
we felt it move scanning
the floorboards for ran-
dom quakes our bloodshot
eyes rolling lost behind
the steam of faulty gas-
masks   but when the
tremoring stopped no one
wanted to go down to see
what was the matter even
though it might mean the
process had after a vig-
il of long years finally
come to its end   we
simply couldn't take the
risk too many of us were
    no longer awake

July 30, 1976

Locusts

to imagine the cloud so low
that all the trees are lost
in its swarm of ashes
you have to forget
the sky is blue

drilling noises
splintered bark
dust over grass
and nettles the
weeds twist un-
derfoot

"there were times we
used to snatch them
out of the air with
our hands
we would tie
them to long pieces
of string and watch
them fly away
if you held on
to the leash a hair
too long the locust

carried you up into
the trees where you
vanished
                I lost four
of my sons that way"

before he turns to exit
you recognize the shag-
gy gray proboscis gnaw-
ing on the wooden spoon

his eyes are redbeads
his wings transparent
with the veining of a
dried-up leaf

August 20, 1976

The Zone

first
we tried to raise up
our heads but it was
no good
too many dead leaves
had come between our
eyes and this forest
was now no more than
the vague setting of
a dream
less to touch and to
hear for it had been
a long time since we
had any fear of com-
ing upon the strange
animal who blew down
the leaves that made
us blind

August 2, 1976

Fading Algebra

pass by slowly

almost nothing
remains of the
light but this

they come down
in secrecy the
shadowbranches
upright in the
wall open bur-
nished coffers
for the burial
of the sardine

July 25, 1976

The Recognition

a room in the dark
possibility of one
who clicks a latch
for as long as the
lamplight absences

above stairs

who would like to see me
just once another non-face
from the wrong side of the
mirror staring into an un-
familiar depth

August 17, 1976

Topology

to begin again
after the dust
ramp fragments
teetering into
smoke   you
search for bones
one stratum rock
piled on another
you carry the dead
city in your belly
down into a crater
a single hair or a
fingernail chip is
enough to make the
ashes rise above the
streets all the emp-
ty houses go black

July 24, 1976

Vox Umbra

billions of years after the
coming of waters the shadow

after primeval light spread
an aurora of blood
  on the dark face
    of the moon
        the shadow was
       then the ocean
  unknown to fathom voices
bubbling from a murky depth
to break its green surfaces
of mist into rippled clouds
wordlessly
mimicked waves
across its soft underbelly
  glimpsed from the deep by
  the one-eyed forebear of
     some forgotten race
the land still a vitreous
blue along the deadly reefs
jagged coves of moss strung
with clods of seaweed dried
to make a curtain for
  the long hibernation
     of the dolphins

there is not an eye nothing
one could call a nose
or a mouth but this
toothless blowhole
of scalloped gums
           jaw enough
      left of my marrow
to keep the passage open at
all hours for gulps of food
and oxygen I am waiting for
the end but the End was
yesterday
           to be sure
    this room was less
than what it has become
full of my own dust and
the noise of far off waters
wandering whispering drying
the dew with the breath
of chemical weeds
           I came to it then
the room if that's what you
still call it I came to the
room then I the man
          with hollow eyes
      with no true mouth
to where no other mouths
could ever find me the mold
to those voices yet to come

this house *if* a house it is

what I came to after long
journeys whispering on
four paws
   shells for hearing
wedded to a depth of candle
wax with half-transparent
fuzz to muffle the empty
distances between
     the oceans
upturned beaches pebble and
rock
that cover all the cities I
have buried this house also
under the mountains of loam

dew clings all these nights
of June are bubbled upside
down in the couchgrass
before a buried sun
appears
   red blotches freckle
the bottom of the sky where
clouds or stars might still
be lying in a fog
     feverish voices
come to the paper long
journeys after whispers
affirming uselessly
   exaggerations they
themselves are unaware of
close to what would be my
sickbed bottles and emptied

                    glass a tarnished teaspoon
                    to keep me calm
                                so I won't know
                    how they are letting me die

                    I can remember ancient ways
                    still but only long enough
                    to keep some fugitive
                    image in
                                the memory
                                from one time
                                to another yes
                            of things seen within
                    the compass of a rubble the
                    debris I must come to again
                    alone by the eyeless method
                    I puzzle out the ruins of
                    buildings or rather
                            the girders of buildings
                    crusted in lime and bubbled
                    tar still fuming the jigsaw
                    of disconnected cities that
                    remake the old horizons
                    too far gone
                                    to spit
                                or shit on all things
                            past that seem like smoke
                    nothing more nothing less I
                    can remember long the night
                    long the days all equally
                    the night
                                heat of the muzzle

blistering dehydrations
in the cavern of the throat
at certain hours of sleep I
glimpse old shadows walking
those other men
with hollow eyes
    whose rounded bills
  still carry the ancient
smile
    the only smile
the night makes over
as they come to take
possession of the night

June 1977

Eric Basso was born in Baltimore in 1947. His work has appeared in *Bakunin*, the *Chicago Review*, *Central Park*, *Collages & Bricolages*, *Fiction International*, *Exquisite Corpse*, and many other publications. His novel, *Bartholomew Fair*, is available from Asylum Arts. He is the author of twenty-one plays. His critically-acclaimed drama trilogy, *The Golem Triptych*; the complete short plays, *Enigmas*; his play, *The Sabattier Effect*; a book of short fiction, *The Beak Doctor*; and five collections of poetry, *Accidental Monsters*, *The Catwalk Watch*, *The Smoking Mirror*, *Catafalques* and *Ghost Light*, are available from Asylum Arts, along with *Decompositions: Essays on Art & Literature 1973–1989* and *Revagaions: 1966–1974*, the first volume of his book of dreams.

Basso's seventh collection of poems, *Earthworks*, was published by Six Gallery Press in 2008.

Leaping Dog Press, featuring Asylum Arts Press

APPLEBAUM, SAMUEL. *Chtcheglov: Poems.* Asylum Arts.
APPLEBAUM, SAMUEL. *Judea Capta: A Long Poem.* Asylum Arts.
AUFDERHEIDE, CHARLES. *Garden of Games: The Collected Poems of Charles E. Aufderheide.* Asylum Arts.
BASSO, ERIC. *Accidental Monsters: Poems & Texts, 1976.* Asylum Arts.
BASSO, ERIC. *Bartholomew Fair: Fiction.* Asylum Arts.
BASSO, ERIC. *The Beak Doctor: Short Fiction, 1972–1976.* Asylum Arts.
BASSO, ERIC. *Catafalques: Poems, 1987–1989.* Asylum Arts.
BASSO, ERIC. *The Catwalk Watch: Poems, 1977–1979.* Asylum Arts.
BASSO, ERIC. *Decompositions: Essays, 1973–1989.* Asylum Arts.
BASSO, ERIC. *Enigmas: Short Plays, 1979–1982.* Asylum Arts.
BASSO, ERIC. *Ghost Light: Poems, 1990–1994.* Asylum Arts.
BASSO, ERIC. *The Golem Triptych: A Dramatic Trilogy.* Asylum Arts.
BASSO, ERIC. *Revagations: A Book of Dreams, 1966–1974.* Asylum Arts.
BASSO, ERIC. *The Sabattier Effect: with incidental music composed & arranged by the author.* Asylum Arts.
BASSO, ERIC. *The Smoking Mirror: Poems, 1980–1986.* Asylum Arts.
BAUDELAIRE, CHARLES. (Kendall Lappin, transl.) *Echoes of Baudelaire: Selected Poems.* Asylum Arts.
BERNARD, KENNETH. *The Baboon in the Nightclub: A Poem.* Asylum Arts.
BERNARD, KENNETH. *How We Danced While We Burned, followed by La Justice, or The Cock That Crew: Two Plays.* Asylum Arts.
BERNARD, KENNETH. *The Qui Parle Play & Poems.* Asylum Arts.
BOYD, GREG. *Carnival Aptitude: Being an Exuberance in Short Prose and Photomontage.* Asylum Arts.
BOYD, GREG. *The Double: Doppelangelgänger: An Annotated Novel.* LDP Book #4.
BOYD, GREG. *The Nambuli Papers: A Multimedia Novel.* LDP Book #6. (Two books, a DVD, and a game)
BOYD, GREG. *Water & Power: Stories.* Asylum Arts.
CULL, MARK E. *One Way Donkey Ride: Short Fiction.* Asylum Arts.
DIXON, STEPHEN. *Friends: More Will and Magna Stories.* Asylum Arts.
DUCORNET, RIKKI. *The Deep Zoo: Two Essays.* LDP Chapbook.
GORDON, KIRPAL. *Eros in Sanskrit: Lyrics & Meditations, 2007–1977.* LDP Book #13.
GORDON, KIRPAL with Music by The Claire Daly Quartet and Special Guests. *Speak-Spake-Spoke.* LDP Media CD.
GORDON, KIRPAL. *What We Got against Tyranny.* LDP Chapbook.
GORDON, KIRPAL. *X Country: Touring the Nation with Jazz & Poetry.* LDP Chapbook.
HENDERSHOT, CYNTHIA. *City of Mazes and Other Tales of Obsession.* Asylum Arts.
HOOD, CHARLES. *The Xopilote Cantos.* Asylum Arts.
JONES, JORDAN. *The Wheel: Poems.* LDP Book #11.

KOSTELANETZ, RICHARD. *Minimal Fictions.* Asylum Arts.
LAPPIN, KENDALL (transl.) *Dead French Poets Speak Plain English: An Anthology of Poetry.* Asylum Arts.
LAPPIN, KENDALL. *Memoirs of a Translator of Poetry.* Asylum Arts.
LAPPIN, KENDALL (transl.). *The Muse Spoke French: An Anthology of Poetry.* Asylum Arts.
MARTIN, JOE. *Parabola: Shorter Fictions.* Asylum Arts.
MARTIN, JOE. *Rumi's Mathnavi: A Play.* Asylum Arts. Forthcoming.
MARTIN, RICHARD. *Marks: Poems.* Asylum Arts.
MARTIN, RICHARD. *Modulations: Poems.* Asylum Arts.
MARTIN, STEPHEN-PAUL. *The Gothic Twilight: Short Fiction.* Asylum Arts.
MARTIN, STEPHEN-PAUL. *Instead of Confusion: Fiction.* Asylum Arts.
NERVAL, GÉRARD DE. (Kendall Lappin, transl., with introduction and notes by ERIC BASSO) *Aurélia, followed by Sylvie: Fiction.* Asylum Arts.
PAPADIMITRAKOPOULOS, ELIAS. *Toothpaste with Chlorophyll & Maritime Hot Baths: Stories.* Asylum Arts.
PETERS, ROBERT. *Mad Ludwig of Bavaria & Other Short Plays: Drama.* Asylum Arts.
PETERS, ROBERT. *Poems: Selected & New 1967–1991.* Asylum Arts.
PETERS, ROBERT. *Where the Bee Sucks: Workers, Drones and Queens of Contemporary American Poetry.* Asylum Arts.
REDONNET, MARIE. (Gilbert Alter-Gilbert, transl.) *Dead Man & Company: Poems.* LDP Book #7.
REDONNET, MARIE. (Jordan Stump, transl.) *Understudies: Stories.* LDP Book #9.
RICHMAN, ELLIOT. *Franz Kafka's Daughter Meets the Evil Nazi Empire!!!: The Heroism of Roaches: Holocaust-tainted Poems.* Asylum Arts.
RICHMAN, ELLIOT. *Honorable Manhood: Poems of Eros & Dust.* Asylum Arts.
RICHMAN, ELLIOT. *The World Dancer: Poems.* Asylum Arts.
RODITI, EDOUARD. *Choose Your Own World.* Asylum Arts.
ROMERO, NORBERTO LUIS. (H. E. Francis, transl.) *Last Night of Carnival & Other Stories.* LDP Book #5.
SHAFFER, ERIC PAUL. *Burn & Learn, or Memoirs of the Cenozoic Era: A Novel.* LDP Book #14.
SHAFFER, ERIC PAUL. *Lāhaina Noon: Nā Mele O Maui: Poems.* LDP Book #10.
SHAFFER, ERIC PAUL. *Living at the Monastery, Working in the Kitchen: Poems.* LDP Book #3.
SHAFFER, ERIC PAUL. *Portable Planet: Poems.* LDP Book #1.
SPRANGER, CHRISTOPHER. *The Comedy of Agony.* LDP Book #12.
STOLOFF, CAROLYN. *You Came to Meet Someone Else: Poems.* Asylum Arts.
TAIT, KIM COPE. *Element: Poems.* LDP Chapbook.
WISNIEWSKI, MARK. *All Weekend with the Lights On: Stories.* LDP Book #2.

Leaping Dog Press / Asylum Arts Press books and *LDP Media* CDs and DVDs are available in fine book and media stores everywhere, on the Internet at leapingdogpress.com, Amazon.com, BN.com, and iTunes, or by contacting:

>Leaping Dog Press, an LDP Media LLC Company
>PO Box 90473
>Raleigh, NC 27675-0473

When ordering direct, include $5 for the first title, and $1.50 for each additional title for shipping. North Carolina residents should add 6.75% sales tax.

Leaping Dog Press / Asylum Arts Press books and e-books are distributed to the trade through:

>**AtlasBooks Distribution**
>30 Amberwood Parkway
>Ashland, OH 44805
>
>**Web:** atlasbooksdistribution.com
>**Phone:** (800) BOOK-LOG / (800) 266-5564
>**Fax:** (419) 281-6883

CDs and digital audio downloads are distributed to the trade through:

>**CD Baby**
>5925 NE 80 Ave
>Portland, OR 97218-2891
>
>**Web:** cdbaby.com
>**Phone:** (503) 595-3000 or (800) BUY-MY-CD
>**Fax:** (503) 296-2370

www.ingramcontent.com/pod-product-compliance
Lightning Source LLC
Chambersburg PA
CBHW022106150426
43195CB00008B/287